Mark Masters Lodge
Book of Marks

Also for
Royal Arch Chapters

Property of

_____ Lodge No._____

_____ Chapter No._____

_____

Volume No. _____

From_____ To_____

by

Comp. James F. Hatcher III

MASONICPRESS.COM

Available from Amazon.com, CreateSpace.com,
and other retail outlets

www.CreateSpace.com/4913627

Printed by CreateSpace, Charleston SC
An Amazon.com Company

Dedicated to
"Hiram, the Builder"

Medieval Masons' Marks

Found on Churches,
Cathedrals and Monuments

*England, Scotland and
Continental Europe*

Directory of Masons' Marks Entered

"A" Surnames

Companion_____ Page_____

Companion_____ Page_____

Companion_____ Page_____

Companion_____ Page_____

Companion_____ Page_____

Companion_____ Page_____

Companion_____ Page_____

Companion_____ Page_____

Companion_____ Page_____

Companion_____ Page_____

Companion_____ Page_____

Companion_____ Page_____

Companion_____ Page_____

Companion_____ Page_____

Companion_____ Page_____

Companion_____ Page_____

Companion_____ Page_____

Companion_____ Page_____

Companion_____ Page_____

Companion_____ Page_____

Directory of Masons' Marks Entered

"A" Surnames

Companion_____ Page_____

Companion_____ Page_____

Companion_____ Page_____

Companion_____ Page_____

Companion_____ Page_____

Companion_____ Page_____

Companion_____ Page_____

Companion_____ Page_____

Companion_____ Page_____

Companion_____ Page_____

Companion_____ Page_____

Companion_____ Page_____

Companion_____ Page_____

Companion_____ Page_____

Companion_____ Page_____

Companion_____ Page_____

Companion_____ Page_____

Companion_____ Page_____

Companion_____ Page_____

Companion_____ Page_____

Directory of Masons' Marks Entered

"A" Surnames

Companion_____ Page_____

Companion_____ Page_____

Companion_____ Page_____

Companion_____ Page_____

Companion_____ Page_____

Companion_____ Page_____

Companion_____ Page_____

Companion_____ Page_____

Companion_____ Page_____

Companion_____ Page_____

Companion_____ Page_____

Companion_____ Page_____

Companion_____ Page_____

Companion_____ Page_____

Companion_____ Page_____

Companion_____ Page_____

Companion_____ Page_____

Companion_____ Page_____

Companion_____ Page_____

Companion_____ Page_____

Directory of Masons' Marks Entered

"A" Surnames

Companion_____ Page_____

Companion_____ Page_____

Companion_____ Page_____

Companion_____ Page_____

Companion_____ Page_____

Companion_____ Page_____

Companion_____ Page_____

Companion_____ Page_____

Companion_____ Page_____

Companion_____ Page_____

Companion_____ Page_____

Companion_____ Page_____

Companion_____ Page_____

Companion_____ Page_____

Companion_____ Page_____

Companion_____ Page_____

Companion_____ Page_____

Companion_____ Page_____

Companion_____ Page_____

Directory of Masons' Marks Entered

"B" Surnames

Companion_____ Page_____

Companion_____ Page_____

Companion_____ Page_____

Companion_____ Page_____

Companion_____ Page_____

Companion_____ Page_____

Companion_____ Page_____

Companion_____ Page_____

Companion_____ Page_____

Companion_____ Page_____

Companion_____ Page_____

Companion_____ Page_____

Companion_____ Page_____

Companion_____ Page_____

Companion_____ Page_____

Companion_____ Page_____

Companion_____ Page_____

Companion_____ Page_____

Companion_____ Page_____

Directory of Masons' Marks Entered

"B" Surnames

Companion_____ Page_____

Companion_____ Page_____

Companion_____ Page_____

Companion_____ Page_____

Companion_____ Page_____

Companion_____ Page_____

Companion_____ Page_____

Companion_____ Page_____

Companion_____ Page_____

Companion_____ Page_____

Companion_____ Page_____

Companion_____ Page_____

Companion_____ Page_____

Companion_____ Page_____

Companion_____ Page_____

Companion_____ Page_____

Companion_____ Page_____

Companion_____ Page_____

Companion_____ Page_____

Directory of Masons' Marks Entered

"B" Surnames

Companion_____ Page_____

Companion_____ Page_____

Companion_____ Page_____

Companion_____ Page_____

Companion_____ Page_____

Companion_____ Page_____

Companion_____ Page_____

Companion_____ Page_____

Companion_____ Page_____

Companion_____ Page_____

Companion_____ Page_____

Companion_____ Page_____

Companion_____ Page_____

Companion_____ Page_____

Companion_____ Page_____

Companion_____ Page_____

Companion_____ Page_____

Companion_____ Page_____

Companion_____ Page_____

Directory of Masons' Marks Entered

"B" Surnames

Companion_____ Page_____

Companion_____ Page_____

Companion_____ Page_____

Companion_____ Page_____

Companion_____ Page_____

Companion_____ Page_____

Companion_____ Page_____

Companion_____ Page_____

Companion_____ Page_____

Companion_____ Page_____

Companion_____ Page_____

Companion_____ Page_____

Companion_____ Page_____

Companion_____ Page_____

Companion_____ Page_____

Companion_____ Page_____

Companion_____ Page_____

Companion_____ Page_____

Companion_____ Page_____

Directory of Masons' Marks Entered

"C" Surnames

Companion_____ Page_____

Companion_____ Page_____

Companion_____ Page_____

Companion_____ Page_____

Companion_____ Page_____

Companion_____ Page_____

Companion_____ Page_____

Companion_____ Page_____

Companion_____ Page_____

Companion_____ Page_____

Companion_____ Page_____

Companion_____ Page_____

Companion_____ Page_____

Companion_____ Page_____

Companion_____ Page_____

Companion_____ Page_____

Companion_____ Page_____

Companion_____ Page_____

Companion_____ Page_____

Directory of Masons' Marks Entered

"C" Surnames

Companion_____ Page_____

Companion_____ Page_____

Companion_____ Page_____

Companion_____ Page_____

Companion_____ Page_____

Companion_____ Page_____

Companion_____ Page_____

Companion_____ Page_____

Companion_____ Page_____

Companion_____ Page_____

Companion_____ Page_____

Companion_____ Page_____

Companion_____ Page_____

Companion_____ Page_____

Companion_____ Page_____

Companion_____ Page_____

Companion_____ Page_____

Companion_____ Page_____

Companion_____ Page_____

Companion_____ Page_____

Directory of Masons' Marks Entered

"C" Surnames

Companion_____ Page_____

Companion_____ Page_____

Companion_____ Page_____

Companion_____ Page_____

Companion_____ Page_____

Companion_____ Page_____

Companion_____ Page_____

Companion_____ Page_____

Companion_____ Page_____

Companion_____ Page_____

Companion_____ Page_____

Companion_____ Page_____

Companion_____ Page_____

Companion_____ Page_____

Companion_____ Page_____

Companion_____ Page_____

Companion_____ Page_____

Companion_____ Page_____

Companion_____ Page_____

Companion_____ Page_____

Directory of Masons' Marks Entered

"C" Surnames

Companion_____ Page_____

Companion_____ Page_____

Companion_____ Page_____

Companion_____ Page_____

Companion_____ Page_____

Companion_____ Page_____

Companion_____ Page_____

Companion_____ Page_____

Companion_____ Page_____

Companion_____ Page_____

Companion_____ Page_____

Companion_____ Page_____

Companion_____ Page_____

Companion_____ Page_____

Companion_____ Page_____

Companion_____ Page_____

Companion_____ Page_____

Companion_____ Page_____

Companion_____ Page_____

Companion_____ Page_____

Directory of Masons' Marks Entered

"D" Surnames

Companion_____ Page_____

Companion_____ Page_____

Companion_____ Page_____

Companion_____ Page_____

Companion_____ Page_____

Companion_____ Page_____

Companion_____ Page_____

Companion_____ Page_____

Companion_____ Page_____

Companion_____ Page_____

Companion_____ Page_____

Companion_____ Page_____

Companion_____ Page_____

Companion_____ Page_____

Companion_____ Page_____

Companion_____ Page_____

Companion_____ Page_____

Companion_____ Page_____

Companion_____ Page_____

Companion_____ Page_____

Directory of Masons' Marks Entered

"D" Surnames

Companion_____ Page_____

Companion_____ Page_____

Companion_____ Page_____

Companion_____ Page_____

Companion_____ Page_____

Companion_____ Page_____

Companion_____ Page_____

Companion_____ Page_____

Companion_____ Page_____

Companion_____ Page_____

Companion_____ Page_____

Companion_____ Page_____

Companion_____ Page_____

Companion_____ Page_____

Companion_____ Page_____

Companion_____ Page_____

Companion_____ Page_____

Companion_____ Page_____

Companion_____ Page_____

Directory of Masons' Marks Entered

"D" Surnames

Companion_____ Page_____

Companion_____ Page_____

Companion_____ Page_____

Companion_____ Page_____

Companion_____ Page_____

Companion_____ Page_____

Companion_____ Page_____

Companion_____ Page_____

Companion_____ Page_____

Companion_____ Page_____

Companion_____ Page_____

Companion_____ Page_____

Companion_____ Page_____

Companion_____ Page_____

Companion_____ Page_____

Companion_____ Page_____

Companion_____ Page_____

Companion_____ Page_____

Companion_____ Page_____

Companion_____ Page_____

Directory of Masons' Marks Entered

"D" Surnames

Companion_____ Page_____

Companion_____ Page_____

Companion_____ Page_____

Companion_____ Page_____

Companion_____ Page_____

Companion_____ Page_____

Companion_____ Page_____

Companion_____ Page_____

Companion_____ Page_____

Companion_____ Page_____

Companion_____ Page_____

Companion_____ Page_____

Companion_____ Page_____

Companion_____ Page_____

Companion_____ Page_____

Companion_____ Page_____

Companion_____ Page_____

Companion_____ Page_____

Companion_____ Page_____

Directory of Masons' Marks Entered

"E" Surnames

Companion_____ Page_____

Companion_____ Page_____

Companion_____ Page_____

Companion_____ Page_____

Companion_____ Page_____

Companion_____ Page_____

Companion_____ Page_____

Companion_____ Page_____

Companion_____ Page_____

Companion_____ Page_____

Companion_____ Page_____

Companion_____ Page_____

Companion_____ Page_____

Companion_____ Page_____

Companion_____ Page_____

Companion_____ Page_____

Companion_____ Page_____

Companion_____ Page_____

Companion_____ Page_____

Companion_____ Page_____

Directory of Masons' Marks Entered

"E" Surnames

Companion_____ Page_____

Companion_____ Page_____

Companion_____ Page_____

Companion_____ Page_____

Companion_____ Page_____

Companion_____ Page_____

Companion_____ Page_____

Companion_____ Page_____

Companion_____ Page_____

Companion_____ Page_____

Companion_____ Page_____

Companion_____ Page_____

Companion_____ Page_____

Companion_____ Page_____

Companion_____ Page_____

Companion_____ Page_____

Companion_____ Page_____

Companion_____ Page_____

Companion_____ Page_____

Directory of Masons' Marks Entered

"E" Surnames

Companion_____ Page_____

Companion_____ Page_____

Companion_____ Page_____

Companion_____ Page_____

Companion_____ Page_____

Companion_____ Page_____

Companion_____ Page_____

Companion_____ Page_____

Companion_____ Page_____

Companion_____ Page_____

Companion_____ Page_____

Companion_____ Page_____

Companion_____ Page_____

Companion_____ Page_____

Companion_____ Page_____

Companion_____ Page_____

Companion_____ Page_____

Companion_____ Page_____

Companion_____ Page_____

Directory of Masons' Marks Entered

"E" Surnames

Companion_____ Page_____

Companion_____ Page_____

Companion_____ Page_____

Companion_____ Page_____

Companion_____ Page_____

Companion_____ Page_____

Companion_____ Page_____

Companion_____ Page_____

Companion_____ Page_____

Companion_____ Page_____

Companion_____ Page_____

Companion_____ Page_____

Companion_____ Page_____

Companion_____ Page_____

Companion_____ Page_____

Companion_____ Page_____

Companion_____ Page_____

Companion_____ Page_____

Companion_____ Page_____

Directory of Masons' Marks Entered

"F" Surnames

Companion_____ Page_____

Companion_____ Page_____

Companion_____ Page_____

Companion_____ Page_____

Companion_____ Page_____

Companion_____ Page_____

Companion_____ Page_____

Companion_____ Page_____

Companion_____ Page_____

Companion_____ Page_____

Companion_____ Page_____

Companion_____ Page_____

Companion_____ Page_____

Companion_____ Page_____

Companion_____ Page_____

Companion_____ Page_____

Companion_____ Page_____

Companion_____ Page_____

Companion_____ Page_____

Companion_____ Page_____

Directory of Masons' Marks Entered

"F" Surnames

Companion_____ Page_____

Companion_____ Page_____

Companion_____ Page_____

Companion_____ Page_____

Companion_____ Page_____

Companion_____ Page_____

Companion_____ Page_____

Companion_____ Page_____

Companion_____ Page_____

Companion_____ Page_____

Companion_____ Page_____

Companion_____ Page_____

Companion_____ Page_____

Companion_____ Page_____

Companion_____ Page_____

Companion_____ Page_____

Companion_____ Page_____

Companion_____ Page_____

Companion_____ Page_____

Directory of Masons' Marks Entered

"F" Surnames

Companion_____ Page_____

Companion_____ Page_____

Companion_____ Page_____

Companion_____ Page_____

Companion_____ Page_____

Companion_____ Page_____

Companion_____ Page_____

Companion_____ Page_____

Companion_____ Page_____

Companion_____ Page_____

Companion_____ Page_____

Companion_____ Page_____

Companion_____ Page_____

Companion_____ Page_____

Companion_____ Page_____

Companion_____ Page_____

Companion_____ Page_____

Companion_____ Page_____

Companion_____ Page_____

Companion_____ Page_____

Directory of Masons' Marks Entered

"F" Surnames

Companion_____ Page_____

Companion_____ Page_____

Companion_____ Page_____

Companion_____ Page_____

Companion_____ Page_____

Companion_____ Page_____

Companion_____ Page_____

Companion_____ Page_____

Companion_____ Page_____

Companion_____ Page_____

Companion_____ Page_____

Companion_____ Page_____

Companion_____ Page_____

Companion_____ Page_____

Companion_____ Page_____

Companion_____ Page_____

Companion_____ Page_____

Companion_____ Page_____

Companion_____ Page_____

Directory of Masons' Marks Entered

"G" Surnames

Companion_____ Page_____

Companion_____ Page_____

Companion_____ Page_____

Companion_____ Page_____

Companion_____ Page_____

Companion_____ Page_____

Companion_____ Page_____

Companion_____ Page_____

Companion_____ Page_____

Companion_____ Page_____

Companion_____ Page_____

Companion_____ Page_____

Companion_____ Page_____

Companion_____ Page_____

Companion_____ Page_____

Companion_____ Page_____

Companion_____ Page_____

Companion_____ Page_____

Companion_____ Page_____

Directory of Masons' Marks Entered

"G" Surnames

Companion_____ Page_____

Companion_____ Page_____

Companion_____ Page_____

Companion_____ Page_____

Companion_____ Page_____

Companion_____ Page_____

Companion_____ Page_____

Companion_____ Page_____

Companion_____ Page_____

Companion_____ Page_____

Companion_____ Page_____

Companion_____ Page_____

Companion_____ Page_____

Companion_____ Page_____

Companion_____ Page_____

Companion_____ Page_____

Companion_____ Page_____

Companion_____ Page_____

Companion_____ Page_____

Companion_____ Page_____

Directory of Masons' Marks Entered

"G" Surnames

Companion_____ Page_____

Companion_____ Page_____

Companion_____ Page_____

Companion_____ Page_____

Companion_____ Page_____

Companion_____ Page_____

Companion_____ Page_____

Companion_____ Page_____

Companion_____ Page_____

Companion_____ Page_____

Companion_____ Page_____

Companion_____ Page_____

Companion_____ Page_____

Companion_____ Page_____

Companion_____ Page_____

Companion_____ Page_____

Companion_____ Page_____

Companion_____ Page_____

Companion_____ Page_____

Companion_____ Page_____

Directory of Masons' Marks Entered

"G" Surnames

Companion_____ Page_____

Companion_____ Page_____

Companion_____ Page_____

Companion_____ Page_____

Companion_____ Page_____

Companion_____ Page_____

Companion_____ Page_____

Companion_____ Page_____

Companion_____ Page_____

Companion_____ Page_____

Companion_____ Page_____

Companion_____ Page_____

Companion_____ Page_____

Companion_____ Page_____

Companion_____ Page_____

Companion_____ Page_____

Companion_____ Page_____

Companion_____ Page_____

Directory of Masons' Marks Entered

"H" Surnames

Companion_____ Page_____

Companion_____ Page_____

Companion_____ Page_____

Companion_____ Page_____

Companion_____ Page_____

Companion_____ Page_____

Companion_____ Page_____

Companion_____ Page_____

Companion_____ Page_____

Companion_____ Page_____

Companion_____ Page_____

Companion_____ Page_____

Companion_____ Page_____

Companion_____ Page_____

Companion_____ Page_____

Companion_____ Page_____

Companion_____ Page_____

Companion_____ Page_____

Companion_____ Page_____

Companion_____ Page_____

Directory of Masons' Marks Entered

"H" Surnames

Companion_____ Page_____

Companion_____ Page_____

Companion_____ Page_____

Companion_____ Page_____

Companion_____ Page_____

Companion_____ Page_____

Companion_____ Page_____

Companion_____ Page_____

Companion_____ Page_____

Companion_____ Page_____

Companion_____ Page_____

Companion_____ Page_____

Companion_____ Page_____

Companion_____ Page_____

Companion_____ Page_____

Companion_____ Page_____

Companion_____ Page_____

Companion_____ Page_____

Companion_____ Page_____

Companion_____ Page_____

Directory of Masons' Marks Entered

"H" Surnames

Companion_____ Page_____

Companion_____ Page_____

Companion_____ Page_____

Companion_____ Page_____

Companion_____ Page_____

Companion_____ Page_____

Companion_____ Page_____

Companion_____ Page_____

Companion_____ Page_____

Companion_____ Page_____

Companion_____ Page_____

Companion_____ Page_____

Companion_____ Page_____

Companion_____ Page_____

Companion_____ Page_____

Companion_____ Page_____

Companion_____ Page_____

Companion_____ Page_____

Companion_____ Page_____

Companion_____ Page_____

Directory of Masons' Marks Entered

"H" Surnames

Companion_____ Page_____

Companion_____ Page_____

Companion_____ Page_____

Companion_____ Page_____

Companion_____ Page_____

Companion_____ Page_____

Companion_____ Page_____

Companion_____ Page_____

Companion_____ Page_____

Companion_____ Page_____

Companion_____ Page_____

Companion_____ Page_____

Companion_____ Page_____

Companion_____ Page_____

Companion_____ Page_____

Companion_____ Page_____

Companion_____ Page_____

Companion_____ Page_____

Companion_____ Page_____

Companion_____ Page_____

Directory of Masons' Marks Entered

"I" Surnames

Companion_____ Page_____

Companion_____ Page_____

Companion_____ Page_____

Companion_____ Page_____

Companion_____ Page_____

Companion_____ Page_____

Companion_____ Page_____

Companion_____ Page_____

Companion_____ Page_____

Companion_____ Page_____

Companion_____ Page_____

Companion_____ Page_____

Companion_____ Page_____

Companion_____ Page_____

Companion_____ Page_____

Companion_____ Page_____

Companion_____ Page_____

Companion_____ Page_____

Companion_____ Page_____

Companion_____ Page_____

Companion_____ Page_____

Directory of Masons' Marks Entered

"I" Surnames

Companion_____ Page_____

Companion_____ Page_____

Companion_____ Page_____

Companion_____ Page_____

Companion_____ Page_____

Companion_____ Page_____

Companion_____ Page_____

Companion_____ Page_____

Companion_____ Page_____

Companion_____ Page_____

Companion_____ Page_____

Companion_____ Page_____

Companion_____ Page_____

Companion_____ Page_____

Companion_____ Page_____

Companion_____ Page_____

Companion_____ Page_____

Companion_____ Page_____

Companion_____ Page_____

Companion_____ Page_____

Directory of Masons' Marks Entered

"I" Surnames

Companion_____ Page_____

Companion_____ Page_____

Companion_____ Page_____

Companion_____ Page_____

Companion_____ Page_____

Companion_____ Page_____

Companion_____ Page_____

Companion_____ Page_____

Companion_____ Page_____

Companion_____ Page_____

Companion_____ Page_____

Companion_____ Page_____

Companion_____ Page_____

Companion_____ Page_____

Companion_____ Page_____

Companion_____ Page_____

Companion_____ Page_____

Companion_____ Page_____

Companion_____ Page_____

Directory of Masons' Marks Entered

"I" Surnames

Companion_____ Page_____

Companion_____ Page_____

Companion_____ Page_____

Companion_____ Page_____

Companion_____ Page_____

Companion_____ Page_____

Companion_____ Page_____

Companion_____ Page_____

Companion_____ Page_____

Companion_____ Page_____

Companion_____ Page_____

Companion_____ Page_____

Companion_____ Page_____

Companion_____ Page_____

Companion_____ Page_____

Companion_____ Page_____

Companion_____ Page_____

Companion_____ Page_____

Companion_____ Page_____

Directory of Masons' Marks Entered

"J" Surnames

Companion_____ Page_____

Companion_____ Page_____

Companion_____ Page_____

Companion_____ Page_____

Companion_____ Page_____

Companion_____ Page_____

Companion_____ Page_____

Companion_____ Page_____

Companion_____ Page_____

Companion_____ Page_____

Companion_____ Page_____

Companion_____ Page_____

Companion_____ Page_____

Companion_____ Page_____

Companion_____ Page_____

Companion_____ Page_____

Companion_____ Page_____

Companion_____ Page_____

Companion_____ Page_____

Companion_____ Page_____

Directory of Masons' Marks Entered

"J" Surnames

Companion_____ Page_____

Companion_____ Page_____

Companion_____ Page_____

Companion_____ Page_____

Companion_____ Page_____

Companion_____ Page_____

Companion_____ Page_____

Companion_____ Page_____

Companion_____ Page_____

Companion_____ Page_____

Companion_____ Page_____

Companion_____ Page_____

Companion_____ Page_____

Companion_____ Page_____

Companion_____ Page_____

Companion_____ Page_____

Companion_____ Page_____

Companion_____ Page_____

Companion_____ Page_____

Companion_____ Page_____

Directory of Masons' Marks Entered

"J" Surnames

Companion_____ Page_____

Companion_____ Page_____

Companion_____ Page_____

Companion_____ Page_____

Companion_____ Page_____

Companion_____ Page_____

Companion_____ Page_____

Companion_____ Page_____

Companion_____ Page_____

Companion_____ Page_____

Companion_____ Page_____

Companion_____ Page_____

Companion_____ Page_____

Companion_____ Page_____

Companion_____ Page_____

Companion_____ Page_____

Companion_____ Page_____

Companion_____ Page_____

Companion_____ Page_____

Companion_____ Page_____

Directory of Masons' Marks Entered

"J" Surnames

Companion_____ Page_____

Companion_____ Page_____

Companion_____ Page_____

Companion_____ Page_____

Companion_____ Page_____

Companion_____ Page_____

Companion_____ Page_____

Companion_____ Page_____

Companion_____ Page_____

Companion_____ Page_____

Companion_____ Page_____

Companion_____ Page_____

Companion_____ Page_____

Companion_____ Page_____

Companion_____ Page_____

Companion_____ Page_____

Companion_____ Page_____

Companion_____ Page_____

Companion_____ Page_____

Companion_____ Page_____

Directory of Masons' Marks Entered

"K" Surnames

Companion_____ Page_____

Companion_____ Page_____

Companion_____ Page_____

Companion_____ Page_____

Companion_____ Page_____

Companion_____ Page_____

Companion_____ Page_____

Companion_____ Page_____

Companion_____ Page_____

Companion_____ Page_____

Companion_____ Page_____

Companion_____ Page_____

Companion_____ Page_____

Companion_____ Page_____

Companion_____ Page_____

Companion_____ Page_____

Companion_____ Page_____

Companion_____ Page_____

Companion_____ Page_____

Companion_____ Page_____

Directory of Masons' Marks Entered

"K" Surnames

Companion_____ Page_____

Companion_____ Page_____

Companion_____ Page_____

Companion_____ Page_____

Companion_____ Page_____

Companion_____ Page_____

Companion_____ Page_____

Companion_____ Page_____

Companion_____ Page_____

Companion_____ Page_____

Companion_____ Page_____

Companion_____ Page_____

Companion_____ Page_____

Companion_____ Page_____

Companion_____ Page_____

Companion_____ Page_____

Companion_____ Page_____

Companion_____ Page_____

Companion_____ Page_____

Directory of Masons' Marks Entered

"K" Surnames

Companion_____ Page_____

Companion_____ Page_____

Companion_____ Page_____

Companion_____ Page_____

Companion_____ Page_____

Companion_____ Page_____

Companion_____ Page_____

Companion_____ Page_____

Companion_____ Page_____

Companion_____ Page_____

Companion_____ Page_____

Companion_____ Page_____

Companion_____ Page_____

Companion_____ Page_____

Companion_____ Page_____

Companion_____ Page_____

Companion_____ Page_____

Companion_____ Page_____

Companion_____ Page_____

Companion_____ Page_____

Directory of Masons' Marks Entered

"K" Surnames

Companion_____ Page_____

Companion_____ Page_____

Companion_____ Page_____

Companion_____ Page_____

Companion_____ Page_____

Companion_____ Page_____

Companion_____ Page_____

Companion_____ Page_____

Companion_____ Page_____

Companion_____ Page_____

Companion_____ Page_____

Companion_____ Page_____

Companion_____ Page_____

Companion_____ Page_____

Companion_____ Page_____

Companion_____ Page_____

Companion_____ Page_____

Companion_____ Page_____

Companion_____ Page_____

Companion_____ Page_____

Directory of Masons' Marks Entered

"L" Surnames

Companion_____ Page_____

Companion_____ Page_____

Companion_____ Page_____

Companion_____ Page_____

Companion_____ Page_____

Companion_____ Page_____

Companion_____ Page_____

Companion_____ Page_____

Companion_____ Page_____

Companion_____ Page_____

Companion_____ Page_____

Companion_____ Page_____

Companion_____ Page_____

Companion_____ Page_____

Companion_____ Page_____

Companion_____ Page_____

Companion_____ Page_____

Companion_____ Page_____

Companion_____ Page_____

Directory of Masons' Marks Entered

"L" Surnames

Companion_____ Page_____

Companion_____ Page_____

Companion_____ Page_____

Companion_____ Page_____

Companion_____ Page_____

Companion_____ Page_____

Companion_____ Page_____

Companion_____ Page_____

Companion_____ Page_____

Companion_____ Page_____

Companion_____ Page_____

Companion_____ Page_____

Companion_____ Page_____

Companion_____ Page_____

Companion_____ Page_____

Companion_____ Page_____

Companion_____ Page_____

Companion_____ Page_____

Companion_____ Page_____

Companion_____ Page_____

Directory of Masons' Marks Entered

"L" Surnames

Companion_____ Page_____

Companion_____ Page_____

Companion_____ Page_____

Companion_____ Page_____

Companion_____ Page_____

Companion_____ Page_____

Companion_____ Page_____

Companion_____ Page_____

Companion_____ Page_____

Companion_____ Page_____

Companion_____ Page_____

Companion_____ Page_____

Companion_____ Page_____

Companion_____ Page_____

Companion_____ Page_____

Companion_____ Page_____

Companion_____ Page_____

Companion_____ Page_____

Companion_____ Page_____

Companion_____ Page

Directory of Masons' Marks Entered

"L" Surnames

Companion_____ Page_____

Companion_____ Page_____

Companion_____ Page_____

Companion_____ Page_____

Companion_____ Page_____

Companion_____ Page_____

Companion_____ Page_____

Companion_____ Page_____

Companion_____ Page_____

Companion_____ Page_____

Companion_____ Page_____

Companion_____ Page_____

Companion_____ Page_____

Companion_____ Page_____

Companion_____ Page_____

Companion_____ Page_____

Companion_____ Page_____

Companion_____ Page_____

Companion_____ Page_____

Directory of Masons' Marks Entered

"M" Surnames

Companion_____ Page_____

Companion_____ Page_____

Companion_____ Page_____

Companion_____ Page_____

Companion_____ Page_____

Companion_____ Page_____

Companion_____ Page_____

Companion_____ Page_____

Companion_____ Page_____

Companion_____ Page_____

Companion_____ Page_____

Companion_____ Page_____

Companion_____ Page_____

Companion_____ Page_____

Companion_____ Page_____

Companion_____ Page_____

Companion_____ Page_____

Companion_____ Page_____

Companion_____ Page_____

Companion_____ Page_____

Directory of Masons' Marks Entered

"M" Surnames

Companion_____ Page_____

Companion_____ Page_____

Companion_____ Page_____

Companion_____ Page_____

Companion_____ Page_____

Companion_____ Page_____

Companion_____ Page_____

Companion_____ Page_____

Companion_____ Page_____

Companion_____ Page_____

Companion_____ Page_____

Companion_____ Page_____

Companion_____ Page_____

Companion_____ Page_____

Companion_____ Page_____

Companion_____ Page_____

Companion_____ Page_____

Companion_____ Page_____

Companion_____ Page_____

Directory of Masons' Marks Entered

"M" Surnames

Companion_____ Page_____

Companion_____ Page_____

Companion_____ Page_____

Companion_____ Page_____

Companion_____ Page_____

Companion_____ Page_____

Companion_____ Page_____

Companion_____ Page_____

Companion_____ Page_____

Companion_____ Page_____

Companion_____ Page_____

Companion_____ Page_____

Companion_____ Page_____

Companion_____ Page_____

Companion_____ Page_____

Companion_____ Page_____

Companion_____ Page_____

Companion_____ Page_____

Companion_____ Page_____

Directory of Masons' Marks Entered

"M" Surnames

Companion_____ Page_____

Companion_____ Page_____

Companion_____ Page_____

Companion_____ Page_____

Companion_____ Page_____

Companion_____ Page_____

Companion_____ Page_____

Companion_____ Page_____

Companion_____ Page_____

Companion_____ Page_____

Companion_____ Page_____

Companion_____ Page_____

Companion_____ Page_____

Companion_____ Page_____

Companion_____ Page_____

Companion_____ Page_____

Companion_____ Page_____

Companion_____ Page_____

Companion_____ Page_____

Companion_____ Page_____

Directory of Masons' Marks Entered

"N" Surnames

Companion_____ Page_____

Companion_____ Page_____

Companion_____ Page_____

Companion_____ Page_____

Companion_____ Page_____

Companion_____ Page_____

Companion_____ Page_____

Companion_____ Page_____

Companion_____ Page_____

Companion_____ Page_____

Companion_____ Page_____

Companion_____ Page_____

Companion_____ Page_____

Companion_____ Page_____

Companion_____ Page_____

Companion_____ Page_____

Companion_____ Page_____

Companion_____ Page_____

Companion_____ Page_____

Directory of Masons' Marks Entered

"N" Surnames

Companion_____ Page_____

Companion_____ Page_____

Companion_____ Page_____

Companion_____ Page_____

Companion_____ Page_____

Companion_____ Page_____

Companion_____ Page_____

Companion_____ Page_____

Companion_____ Page_____

Companion_____ Page_____

Companion_____ Page_____

Companion_____ Page_____

Companion_____ Page_____

Companion_____ Page_____

Companion_____ Page_____

Companion_____ Page_____

Companion_____ Page_____

Companion_____ Page_____

Companion_____ Page_____

Directory of Masons' Marks Entered

"N" Surnames

Companion_____ Page_____

Companion_____ Page_____

Companion_____ Page_____

Companion_____ Page_____

Companion_____ Page_____

Companion_____ Page_____

Companion_____ Page_____

Companion_____ Page_____

Companion_____ Page_____

Companion_____ Page_____

Companion_____ Page_____

Companion_____ Page_____

Companion_____ Page_____

Companion_____ Page_____

Companion_____ Page_____

Companion_____ Page_____

Companion_____ Page_____

Companion_____ Page_____

Companion_____ Page_____

Companion_____ Page_____

Directory of Masons' Marks Entered

"N" Surnames

Companion_____ Page_____

Companion_____ Page_____

Companion_____ Page_____

Companion_____ Page_____

Companion_____ Page_____

Companion_____ Page_____

Companion_____ Page_____

Companion_____ Page_____

Companion_____ Page_____

Companion_____ Page_____

Companion_____ Page_____

Companion_____ Page_____

Companion_____ Page_____

Companion_____ Page_____

Companion_____ Page_____

Companion_____ Page_____

Companion_____ Page_____

Companion_____ Page_____

Companion_____ Page_____

Directory of Masons' Marks Entered

"O" Surnames

Companion_____ Page_____

Companion_____ Page_____

Companion_____ Page_____

Companion_____ Page_____

Companion_____ Page_____

Companion_____ Page_____

Companion_____ Page_____

Companion_____ Page_____

Companion_____ Page_____

Companion_____ Page_____

Companion_____ Page_____

Companion_____ Page_____

Companion_____ Page_____

Companion_____ Page_____

Companion_____ Page_____

Companion_____ Page_____

Companion_____ Page_____

Companion_____ Page_____

Companion_____ Page_____

Companion_____ Page_____

Directory of Masons' Marks Entered

"O" Surnames

Companion_____ Page_____

Companion_____ Page_____

Companion_____ Page_____

Companion_____ Page_____

Companion_____ Page_____

Companion_____ Page_____

Companion_____ Page_____

Companion_____ Page_____

Companion_____ Page_____

Companion_____ Page_____

Companion_____ Page_____

Companion_____ Page_____

Companion_____ Page_____

Companion_____ Page_____

Companion_____ Page_____

Companion_____ Page_____

Companion_____ Page_____

Companion_____ Page_____

Directory of Masons' Marks Entered

"O" Surnames

Companion_____ Page_____

Companion_____ Page_____

Companion_____ Page_____

Companion_____ Page_____

Companion_____ Page_____

Companion_____ Page_____

Companion_____ Page_____

Companion_____ Page_____

Companion_____ Page_____

Companion_____ Page_____

Companion_____ Page_____

Companion_____ Page_____

Companion_____ Page_____

Companion_____ Page_____

Companion_____ Page_____

Companion_____ Page_____

Companion_____ Page_____

Companion_____ Page_____

Companion_____ Page_____

Companion_____ Page_____

Directory of Masons' Marks Entered

"O" Surnames

Companion_____ Page_____

Companion_____ Page_____

Companion_____ Page_____

Companion_____ Page_____

Companion_____ Page_____

Companion_____ Page_____

Companion_____ Page_____

Companion_____ Page_____

Companion_____ Page_____

Companion_____ Page_____

Companion_____ Page_____

Companion_____ Page_____

Companion_____ Page_____

Companion_____ Page_____

Companion_____ Page_____

Companion_____ Page_____

Companion_____ Page_____

Companion_____ Page_____

Companion_____ Page_____

Directory of Masons' Marks Entered

"P" Surnames

Companion_____ Page_____

Companion_____ Page_____

Companion_____ Page_____

Companion_____ Page_____

Companion_____ Page_____

Companion_____ Page_____

Companion_____ Page_____

Companion_____ Page_____

Companion_____ Page_____

Companion_____ Page_____

Companion_____ Page_____

Companion_____ Page_____

Companion_____ Page_____

Companion_____ Page_____

Companion_____ Page_____

Companion_____ Page_____

Companion_____ Page_____

Companion_____ Page_____

Companion_____ Page_____

Directory of Masons' Marks Entered

"P" Surnames

Companion_____ Page_____

Companion_____ Page_____

Companion_____ Page_____

Companion_____ Page_____

Companion_____ Page_____

Companion_____ Page_____

Companion_____ Page_____

Companion_____ Page_____

Companion_____ Page_____

Companion_____ Page_____

Companion_____ Page_____

Companion_____ Page_____

Companion_____ Page_____

Companion_____ Page_____

Companion_____ Page_____

Companion_____ Page_____

Companion_____ Page_____

Companion_____ Page_____

Companion_____ Page_____

Directory of Masons' Marks Entered

"P" Surnames

Companion_____ Page_____

Companion_____ Page_____

Companion_____ Page_____

Companion_____ Page_____

Companion_____ Page_____

Companion_____ Page_____

Companion_____ Page_____

Companion_____ Page_____

Companion_____ Page_____

Companion_____ Page_____

Companion_____ Page_____

Companion_____ Page_____

Companion_____ Page_____

Companion_____ Page_____

Companion_____ Page_____

Companion_____ Page_____

Companion_____ Page_____

Companion_____ Page_____

Companion_____ Page_____

Companion_____ Page_____

Directory of Masons' Marks Entered

"P" Surnames

Companion_____ Page_____

Companion_____ Page_____

Companion_____ Page_____

Companion_____ Page_____

Companion_____ Page_____

Companion_____ Page_____

Companion_____ Page_____

Companion_____ Page_____

Companion_____ Page_____

Companion_____ Page_____

Companion_____ Page_____

Companion_____ Page_____

Companion_____ Page_____

Companion_____ Page_____

Companion_____ Page_____

Companion_____ Page_____

Companion_____ Page_____

Companion_____ Page_____

Companion_____ Page_____

Directory of Masons' Marks Entered

"Q" Surnames

Companion_____ Page_____

Companion_____ Page_____

Companion_____ Page_____

Companion_____ Page_____

Companion_____ Page_____

Companion_____ Page_____

Companion_____ Page_____

Companion_____ Page_____

Companion_____ Page_____

Companion_____ Page_____

Companion_____ Page_____

Companion_____ Page_____

Companion_____ Page_____

Companion_____ Page_____

Companion_____ Page_____

Companion_____ Page_____

Companion_____ Page_____

Companion_____ Page_____

Companion_____ Page_____

Directory of Masons' Marks Entered

"Q" Surnames

Companion_____ Page_____

Companion_____ Page_____

Companion_____ Page_____

Companion_____ Page_____

Companion_____ Page_____

Companion_____ Page_____

Companion_____ Page_____

Companion_____ Page_____

Companion_____ Page_____

Companion_____ Page_____

Companion_____ Page_____

Companion_____ Page_____

Companion_____ Page_____

Companion_____ Page_____

Companion_____ Page_____

Companion_____ Page_____

Companion_____ Page_____

Companion_____ Page_____

Companion_____ Page_____

Directory of Masons' Marks Entered

"Q" Surnames

Companion_____ Page_____

Companion_____ Page_____

Companion_____ Page_____

Companion_____ Page_____

Companion_____ Page_____

Companion_____ Page_____

Companion_____ Page_____

Companion_____ Page_____

Companion_____ Page_____

Companion_____ Page_____

Companion_____ Page_____

Companion_____ Page_____

Companion_____ Page_____

Companion_____ Page_____

Companion_____ Page_____

Companion_____ Page_____

Companion_____ Page_____

Companion_____ Page_____

Companion_____ Page_____

Companion_____ Page_____

Directory of Masons' Marks Entered

"Q" Surnames

Companion_____ Page_____

Companion_____ Page_____

Companion_____ Page_____

Companion_____ Page_____

Companion_____ Page_____

Companion_____ Page_____

Companion_____ Page_____

Companion_____ Page_____

Companion_____ Page_____

Companion_____ Page_____

Companion_____ Page_____

Companion_____ Page_____

Companion_____ Page_____

Companion_____ Page_____

Companion_____ Page_____

Companion_____ Page_____

Companion_____ Page_____

Companion_____ Page_____

Companion_____ Page_____

Directory of Masons' Marks Entered

"R" Surnames

Companion_____ Page_____

Companion_____ Page_____

Companion_____ Page_____

Companion_____ Page_____

Companion_____ Page_____

Companion_____ Page_____

Companion_____ Page_____

Companion_____ Page_____

Companion_____ Page_____

Companion_____ Page_____

Companion_____ Page_____

Companion_____ Page_____

Companion_____ Page_____

Companion_____ Page_____

Companion_____ Page_____

Companion_____ Page_____

Companion_____ Page_____

Companion_____ Page_____

Companion_____ Page_____

Directory of Masons' Marks Entered

"R" Surnames

Companion_____ Page_____

Companion_____ Page_____

Companion_____ Page_____

Companion_____ Page_____

Companion_____ Page_____

Companion_____ Page_____

Companion_____ Page_____

Companion_____ Page_____

Companion_____ Page_____

Companion_____ Page_____

Companion_____ Page_____

Companion_____ Page_____

Companion_____ Page_____

Companion_____ Page_____

Companion_____ Page_____

Companion_____ Page_____

Companion_____ Page_____

Companion_____ Page_____

Companion_____ Page_____

Companion_____ Page_____

Directory of Masons' Marks Entered

"R" Surnames

Companion_____ Page_____

Companion_____ Page_____

Companion_____ Page_____

Companion_____ Page_____

Companion_____ Page_____

Companion_____ Page_____

Companion_____ Page_____

Companion_____ Page_____

Companion_____ Page_____

Companion_____ Page_____

Companion_____ Page_____

Companion_____ Page_____

Companion_____ Page_____

Companion_____ Page_____

Companion_____ Page_____

Companion_____ Page_____

Companion_____ Page_____

Companion_____ Page_____

Companion_____ Page_____

Directory of Masons' Marks Entered

"R" Surnames

Companion_____ Page_____

Companion_____ Page_____

Companion_____ Page_____

Companion_____ Page_____

Companion_____ Page_____

Companion_____ Page_____

Companion_____ Page_____

Companion_____ Page_____

Companion_____ Page_____

Companion_____ Page_____

Companion_____ Page_____

Companion_____ Page_____

Companion_____ Page_____

Companion_____ Page_____

Companion_____ Page_____

Companion_____ Page_____

Companion_____ Page_____

Companion_____ Page_____

Companion_____ Page_____

Directory of Masons' Marks Entered

"S" Surnames

Companion_____ Page_____

Companion_____ Page_____

Companion_____ Page_____

Companion_____ Page_____

Companion_____ Page_____

Companion_____ Page_____

Companion_____ Page_____

Companion_____ Page_____

Companion_____ Page_____

Companion_____ Page_____

Companion_____ Page_____

Companion_____ Page_____

Companion_____ Page_____

Companion_____ Page_____

Companion_____ Page_____

Companion_____ Page_____

Companion_____ Page_____

Companion_____ Page_____

Companion_____ Page_____

Companion_____ Page_____

Directory of Masons' Marks Entered

"S" Surnames

Companion_____ Page_____

Companion_____ Page_____

Companion_____ Page_____

Companion_____ Page_____

Companion_____ Page_____

Companion_____ Page_____

Companion_____ Page_____

Companion_____ Page_____

Companion_____ Page_____

Companion_____ Page_____

Companion_____ Page_____

Companion_____ Page_____

Companion_____ Page_____

Companion_____ Page_____

Companion_____ Page_____

Companion_____ Page_____

Companion_____ Page_____

Companion_____ Page_____

Companion_____ Page_____

Companion_____ Page_____

Directory of Masons' Marks Entered

"S" Surnames

Companion_____ Page_____

Companion_____ Page_____

Companion_____ Page_____

Companion_____ Page_____

Companion_____ Page_____

Companion_____ Page_____

Companion_____ Page_____

Companion_____ Page_____

Companion_____ Page_____

Companion_____ Page_____

Companion_____ Page_____

Companion_____ Page_____

Companion_____ Page_____

Companion_____ Page_____

Companion_____ Page_____

Companion_____ Page_____

Companion_____ Page_____

Companion_____ Page_____

Companion_____ Page_____

Companion_____ Page_____

Directory of Masons' Marks Entered

"S" Surnames

Companion_____ Page_____

Companion_____ Page_____

Companion_____ Page_____

Companion_____ Page_____

Companion_____ Page_____

Companion_____ Page_____

Companion_____ Page_____

Companion_____ Page_____

Companion_____ Page_____

Companion_____ Page_____

Companion_____ Page_____

Companion_____ Page_____

Companion_____ Page_____

Companion_____ Page_____

Companion_____ Page_____

Companion_____ Page_____

Companion_____ Page_____

Companion_____ Page_____

Companion_____ Page_____

Directory of Masons' Marks Entered

"T" Surnames

Companion_____ Page_____

Companion_____ Page_____

Companion_____ Page_____

Companion_____ Page_____

Companion_____ Page_____

Companion_____ Page_____

Companion_____ Page_____

Companion_____ Page_____

Companion_____ Page_____

Companion_____ Page_____

Companion_____ Page_____

Companion_____ Page_____

Companion_____ Page_____

Companion_____ Page_____

Companion_____ Page_____

Companion_____ Page_____

Companion_____ Page_____

Companion_____ Page_____

Companion_____ Page_____

Companion_____ Page_____

Directory of Masons' Marks Entered

"T" Surnames

Companion_____ Page_____

Companion_____ Page_____

Companion_____ Page_____

Companion_____ Page_____

Companion_____ Page_____

Companion_____ Page_____

Companion_____ Page_____

Companion_____ Page_____

Companion_____ Page_____

Companion_____ Page_____

Companion_____ Page_____

Companion_____ Page_____

Companion_____ Page_____

Companion_____ Page_____

Companion_____ Page_____

Companion_____ Page_____

Companion_____ Page_____

Companion_____ Page_____

Companion_____ Page_____

Directory of Masons' Marks Entered

"T" Surnames

Companion_____ Page_____

Companion_____ Page_____

Companion_____ Page_____

Companion_____ Page_____

Companion_____ Page_____

Companion_____ Page_____

Companion_____ Page_____

Companion_____ Page_____

Companion_____ Page_____

Companion_____ Page_____

Companion_____ Page_____

Companion_____ Page_____

Companion_____ Page_____

Companion_____ Page_____

Companion_____ Page_____

Companion_____ Page_____

Companion_____ Page_____

Companion_____ Page_____

Companion_____ Page_____

Directory of Masons' Marks Entered

"T" Surnames

Companion_____ Page_____

Companion_____ Page_____

Companion_____ Page_____

Companion_____ Page_____

Companion_____ Page_____

Companion_____ Page_____

Companion_____ Page_____

Companion_____ Page_____

Companion_____ Page_____

Companion_____ Page_____

Companion_____ Page_____

Companion_____ Page_____

Companion_____ Page_____

Companion_____ Page_____

Companion_____ Page_____

Companion_____ Page_____

Companion_____ Page_____

Companion_____ Page_____

Companion_____ Page_____

Companion_____ Page_____

Directory of Masons' Marks Entered

"U" Surnames

Companion_____ Page_____

Companion_____ Page_____

Companion_____ Page_____

Companion_____ Page_____

Companion_____ Page_____

Companion_____ Page_____

Companion_____ Page_____

Companion_____ Page_____

Companion_____ Page_____

Companion_____ Page_____

Companion_____ Page_____

Companion_____ Page_____

Companion_____ Page_____

Companion_____ Page_____

Companion_____ Page_____

Companion_____ Page_____

Companion_____ Page_____

Companion_____ Page_____

Companion_____ Page_____

Companion_____ Page_____

Directory of Masons' Marks Entered

"U" Surnames

Companion_____ Page_____

Companion_____ Page_____

Companion_____ Page_____

Companion_____ Page_____

Companion_____ Page_____

Companion_____ Page_____

Companion_____ Page_____

Companion_____ Page_____

Companion_____ Page_____

Companion_____ Page_____

Companion_____ Page_____

Companion_____ Page_____

Companion_____ Page_____

Companion_____ Page_____

Companion_____ Page_____

Companion_____ Page_____

Companion_____ Page_____

Companion_____ Page_____

Companion_____ Page_____

Directory of Masons' Marks Entered

"U" Surnames

Companion_____ Page_____

Companion_____ Page_____

Companion_____ Page_____

Companion_____ Page_____

Companion_____ Page_____

Companion_____ Page_____

Companion_____ Page_____

Companion_____ Page_____

Companion_____ Page_____

Companion_____ Page_____

Companion_____ Page_____

Companion_____ Page_____

Companion_____ Page_____

Companion_____ Page_____

Companion_____ Page_____

Companion_____ Page_____

Companion_____ Page_____

Companion_____ Page_____

Companion_____ Page_____

Directory of Masons' Marks Entered

"U" Surnames

Companion_____ Page_____

Companion_____ Page_____

Companion_____ Page_____

Companion_____ Page_____

Companion_____ Page_____

Companion_____ Page_____

Companion_____ Page_____

Companion_____ Page_____

Companion_____ Page_____

Companion_____ Page_____

Companion_____ Page_____

Companion_____ Page_____

Companion_____ Page_____

Companion_____ Page_____

Companion_____ Page_____

Companion_____ Page_____

Companion_____ Page_____

Companion_____ Page_____

Companion_____ Page_____

Companion_____ Page_____

Directory of Masons' Marks Entered

"V" Surnames

Companion_____ Page_____

Companion_____ Page_____

Companion_____ Page_____

Companion_____ Page_____

Companion_____ Page_____

Companion_____ Page_____

Companion_____ Page_____

Companion_____ Page_____

Companion_____ Page_____

Companion_____ Page_____

Companion_____ Page_____

Companion_____ Page_____

Companion_____ Page_____

Companion_____ Page_____

Companion_____ Page_____

Companion_____ Page_____

Companion_____ Page_____

Companion_____ Page_____

Companion_____ Page_____

Companion_____ Page_____

Directory of Masons' Marks Entered

"V" Surnames

Companion_____ Page_____

Companion_____ Page_____

Companion_____ Page_____

Companion_____ Page_____

Companion_____ Page_____

Companion_____ Page_____

Companion_____ Page_____

Companion_____ Page_____

Companion_____ Page_____

Companion_____ Page_____

Companion_____ Page_____

Companion_____ Page_____

Companion_____ Page_____

Companion_____ Page_____

Companion_____ Page_____

Companion_____ Page_____

Companion_____ Page_____

Companion_____ Page_____

Companion_____ Page_____

Directory of Masons' Marks Entered

"V" Surnames

Companion_____ Page_____

Companion_____ Page_____

Companion_____ Page_____

Companion_____ Page_____

Companion_____ Page_____

Companion_____ Page_____

Companion_____ Page_____

Companion_____ Page_____

Companion_____ Page_____

Companion_____ Page_____

Companion_____ Page_____

Companion_____ Page_____

Companion_____ Page_____

Companion_____ Page_____

Companion_____ Page_____

Companion_____ Page_____

Companion_____ Page_____

Companion_____ Page_____

Companion_____ Page_____

Directory of Masons' Marks Entered

"V" Surnames

Companion_____ Page_____

Companion_____ Page_____

Companion_____ Page_____

Companion_____ Page_____

Companion_____ Page_____

Companion_____ Page_____

Companion_____ Page_____

Companion_____ Page_____

Companion_____ Page_____

Companion_____ Page_____

Companion_____ Page_____

Companion_____ Page_____

Companion_____ Page_____

Companion_____ Page_____

Companion_____ Page_____

Companion_____ Page_____

Companion_____ Page_____

Companion_____ Page_____

Companion_____ Page_____

Companion_____ Page_____

Directory of Masons' Marks Entered

"W" Surnames

Companion_____ Page_____

Companion_____ Page_____

Companion_____ Page_____

Companion_____ Page_____

Companion_____ Page_____

Companion_____ Page_____

Companion_____ Page_____

Companion_____ Page_____

Companion_____ Page_____

Companion_____ Page_____

Companion_____ Page_____

Companion_____ Page_____

Companion_____ Page_____

Companion_____ Page_____

Companion_____ Page_____

Companion_____ Page_____

Companion_____ Page_____

Companion_____ Page_____

Companion_____ Page_____

Directory of Masons' Marks Entered

"W" Surnames

Companion_____ Page_____

Companion_____ Page_____

Companion_____ Page_____

Companion_____ Page_____

Companion_____ Page_____

Companion_____ Page_____

Companion_____ Page_____

Companion_____ Page_____

Companion_____ Page_____

Companion_____ Page_____

Companion_____ Page_____

Companion_____ Page_____

Companion_____ Page_____

Companion_____ Page_____

Companion_____ Page_____

Companion_____ Page_____

Companion_____ Page_____

Companion_____ Page_____

Companion_____ Page_____

Companion_____ Page_____

Directory of Masons' Marks Entered

"W" Surnames

Companion_____ Page_____

Companion_____ Page_____

Companion_____ Page_____

Companion_____ Page_____

Companion_____ Page_____

Companion_____ Page_____

Companion_____ Page_____

Companion_____ Page_____

Companion_____ Page_____

Companion_____ Page_____

Companion_____ Page_____

Companion_____ Page_____

Companion_____ Page_____

Companion_____ Page_____

Companion_____ Page_____

Companion_____ Page_____

Companion_____ Page_____

Companion_____ Page_____

Companion_____ Page_____

Directory of Masons' Marks Entered

"W" Surnames

Companion_____ Page_____

Companion_____ Page_____

Companion_____ Page_____

Companion_____ Page_____

Companion_____ Page_____

Companion_____ Page_____

Companion_____ Page_____

Companion_____ Page_____

Companion_____ Page_____

Companion_____ Page_____

Companion_____ Page_____

Companion_____ Page_____

Companion_____ Page_____

Companion_____ Page_____

Companion_____ Page_____

Companion_____ Page_____

Companion_____ Page_____

Companion_____ Page_____

Directory of Masons' Marks Entered

"X" Surnames

Companion_____ Page_____

Companion_____ Page_____

Companion_____ Page_____

Companion_____ Page_____

Companion_____ Page_____

Companion_____ Page_____

Companion_____ Page_____

Companion_____ Page_____

Companion_____ Page_____

Companion_____ Page_____

Companion_____ Page_____

Companion_____ Page_____

Companion_____ Page_____

Companion_____ Page_____

Companion_____ Page_____

Companion_____ Page_____

Companion_____ Page_____

Companion_____ Page_____

Companion_____ Page_____

Companion_____ Page_____

Directory of Masons' Marks Entered

"X" Surnames

Companion_____ Page_____

Companion_____ Page_____

Companion_____ Page_____

Companion_____ Page_____

Companion_____ Page_____

Companion_____ Page_____

Companion_____ Page_____

Companion_____ Page_____

Companion_____ Page_____

Companion_____ Page_____

Companion_____ Page_____

Companion_____ Page_____

Companion_____ Page_____

Companion_____ Page_____

Companion_____ Page_____

Companion_____ Page_____

Companion_____ Page_____

Companion_____ Page_____

Companion_____ Page_____

Directory of Masons' Marks Entered

"X" Surnames

Companion_____ Page_____

Companion_____ Page_____

Companion_____ Page_____

Companion_____ Page_____

Companion_____ Page_____

Companion_____ Page_____

Companion_____ Page_____

Companion_____ Page_____

Companion_____ Page_____

Companion_____ Page_____

Companion_____ Page_____

Companion_____ Page_____

Companion_____ Page_____

Companion_____ Page_____

Companion_____ Page_____

Companion_____ Page_____

Companion_____ Page_____

Companion_____ Page_____

Companion_____ Page_____

Companion_____ Page_____

Directory of Masons' Marks Entered

"X" Surnames

Companion_____ Page_____

Companion_____ Page_____

Companion_____ Page_____

Companion_____ Page_____

Companion_____ Page_____

Companion_____ Page_____

Companion_____ Page_____

Companion_____ Page_____

Companion_____ Page_____

Companion_____ Page_____

Companion_____ Page_____

Companion_____ Page_____

Companion_____ Page_____

Companion_____ Page_____

Companion_____ Page_____

Companion_____ Page_____

Companion_____ Page_____

Companion_____ Page_____

Companion_____ Page_____

Directory of Masons' Marks Entered

"Y" Surnames

Companion_____ Page_____

Companion_____ Page_____

Companion_____ Page_____

Companion_____ Page_____

Companion_____ Page_____

Companion_____ Page_____

Companion_____ Page_____

Companion_____ Page_____

Companion_____ Page_____

Companion_____ Page_____

Companion_____ Page_____

Companion_____ Page_____

Companion_____ Page_____

Companion_____ Page_____

Companion_____ Page_____

Companion_____ Page_____

Companion_____ Page_____

Companion_____ Page_____

Companion_____ Page_____

Directory of Masons' Marks Entered

"Y" Surnames

Companion_____ Page_____

Companion_____ Page_____

Companion_____ Page_____

Companion_____ Page_____

Companion_____ Page_____

Companion_____ Page_____

Companion_____ Page_____

Companion_____ Page_____

Companion_____ Page_____

Companion_____ Page_____

Companion_____ Page_____

Companion_____ Page_____

Companion_____ Page_____

Companion_____ Page_____

Companion_____ Page_____

Companion_____ Page_____

Companion_____ Page_____

Companion_____ Page_____

Companion_____ Page_____

Companion_____ Page_____

Directory of Masons' Marks Entered

"Y" Surnames

Companion_____ Page_____

Companion_____ Page_____

Companion_____ Page_____

Companion_____ Page_____

Companion_____ Page_____

Companion_____ Page_____

Companion_____ Page_____

Companion_____ Page_____

Companion_____ Page_____

Companion_____ Page_____

Companion_____ Page_____

Companion_____ Page_____

Companion_____ Page_____

Companion_____ Page_____

Companion_____ Page_____

Companion_____ Page_____

Companion_____ Page_____

Companion_____ Page_____

Companion_____ Page_____

Companion_____ Page_____

Directory of Masons' Marks Entered

"Y" Surnames

Companion_____ Page_____

Companion_____ Page_____

Companion_____ Page_____

Companion_____ Page_____

Companion_____ Page_____

Companion_____ Page_____

Companion_____ Page_____

Companion_____ Page_____

Companion_____ Page_____

Companion_____ Page_____

Companion_____ Page_____

Companion_____ Page_____

Companion_____ Page_____

Companion_____ Page_____

Companion_____ Page_____

Companion_____ Page_____

Companion_____ Page_____

Companion_____ Page_____

Companion_____ Page_____

Companion_____ Page_____

Directory of Masons' Marks Entered

"Z" Surnames

Companion_____ Page_____

Companion_____ Page_____

Companion_____ Page_____

Companion_____ Page_____

Companion_____ Page_____

Companion_____ Page_____

Companion_____ Page_____

Companion_____ Page_____

Companion_____ Page_____

Companion_____ Page_____

Companion_____ Page_____

Companion_____ Page_____

Companion_____ Page_____

Companion_____ Page_____

Companion_____ Page_____

Companion_____ Page_____

Companion_____ Page_____

Companion_____ Page_____

Companion_____ Page_____

Companion_____ Page_____

Directory of Masons' Marks Entered

"Z" Surnames

Companion_____ Page_____

Companion_____ Page_____

Companion_____ Page_____

Companion_____ Page_____

Companion_____ Page_____

Companion_____ Page_____

Companion_____ Page_____

Companion_____ Page_____

Companion_____ Page_____

Companion_____ Page_____

Companion_____ Page_____

Companion_____ Page_____

Companion_____ Page_____

Companion_____ Page_____

Companion_____ Page_____

Companion_____ Page_____

Companion_____ Page_____

Companion_____ Page_____

Companion_____ Page_____

Directory of Masons' Marks Entered

"Z" Surnames

Companion_____ Page_____

Companion_____ Page_____

Companion_____ Page_____

Companion_____ Page_____

Companion_____ Page_____

Companion_____ Page_____

Companion_____ Page_____

Companion_____ Page_____

Companion_____ Page_____

Companion_____ Page_____

Companion_____ Page_____

Companion_____ Page_____

Companion_____ Page_____

Companion_____ Page_____

Companion_____ Page_____

Companion_____ Page_____

Companion_____ Page_____

Companion_____ Page_____

Companion_____ Page_____

Directory of Masons' Marks Entered

"Z" Surnames

Companion_____ Page_____

Companion_____ Page_____

Companion_____ Page_____

Companion_____ Page_____

Companion_____ Page_____

Companion_____ Page_____

Companion_____ Page_____

Companion_____ Page_____

Companion_____ Page_____

Companion_____ Page_____

Companion_____ Page_____

Companion_____ Page_____

Companion_____ Page_____

Companion_____ Page_____

Companion_____ Page_____

Companion_____ Page_____

Companion_____ Page_____

Companion_____ Page_____

Companion_____ Page_____

Mark Adopted_____

_____
Companion

Mark Adopted_____

_____
Companion

Mark Adopted_____

_____
Companion

Mark Adopted_____

_____
Companion

Mark Adopted_____

_____
Companion

Mark Adopted_____

_____
Companion

Mark Adopted_____

_____
Companion

Mark Adopted_____

_____
Companion

Mark Adopted_____

_____
Companion

Mark Adopted_____

_____
Companion

Mark Adopted_____

_____
Companion

Mark Adopted_____

_____
Companion

Mark Adopted_____

_____
Companion

Mark Adopted_____

_____
Companion

Mark Adopted_____

_____
Companion

Mark Adopted_____

_____
Companion

Mark Adopted_____

_____
Companion

Mark Adopted_____

_____
Companion

Mark Adopted_____

_____
Companion

Mark Adopted_____

_____
Companion

Mark Adopted_____

_____
Companion

Mark Adopted_____

_____
Companion

Mark Adopted_____

_____
Companion

Mark Adopted_____

_____
Companion

Mark Adopted_____

_____
Companion

Mark Adopted_____

_____
Companion

Mark Adopted_____

_____
Companion

Mark Adopted_____

_____
Companion

Mark Adopted_____

_____
Companion

Mark Adopted_____

_____
Companion

Mark Adopted_____

_____
Companion

Mark Adopted_____

_____
Companion

Mark Adopted_____

_____
Companion

Mark Adopted_____

_____
Companion

Mark Adopted_____

_____
Companion

Mark Adopted_____

_____
Companion

Mark Adopted_____

_____
Companion

Mark Adopted_____

_____
Companion

Mark Adopted_____

_____
Companion

Mark Adopted_____

_____
Companion

Mark Adopted_____

_____
Companion

Mark Adopted_____

_____
Companion

Mark Adopted_____

_____
Companion

Mark Adopted_____

_____
Companion

Mark Adopted_____

_____
Companion

Mark Adopted_____

_____
Companion

Mark Adopted_____

_____
Companion

Mark Adopted_____

_____
Companion

Mark Adopted_____

_____
Companion

Mark Adopted_____

_____
Companion

Mark Adopted_____

_____
Companion

Mark Adopted_____

_____
Companion

Mark Adopted_____

_____
Companion

Mark Adopted_____

_____
Companion

Mark Adopted_____

_____
Companion

Mark Adopted_____

_____
Companion

Mark Adopted_____

_____
Companion

Mark Adopted_____

_____
Companion

Mark Adopted_____

_____
Companion

Mark Adopted_____

_____
Companion

Mark Adopted_____

_____
Companion

Mark Adopted_____

_____
Companion

Mark Adopted_____

_____
Companion

Mark Adopted_____

_____
Companion

Mark Adopted_____

_____
Companion

Mark Adopted_____

_____
Companion

Mark Adopted_____

_____
Companion

Mark Adopted_____

_____
Companion

Mark Adopted_____

_____
Companion

Mark Adopted_____

_____
Companion

Mark Adopted_____

_____
Companion

Mark Adopted_____

_____
Companion

Mark Adopted_____

_____
Companion

Mark Adopted_____

_____
Companion

Mark Adopted_____

_____
Companion

Mark Adopted_____

_____
Companion

Mark Adopted_____

_____
Companion

Mark Adopted_____

_____
Companion

Mark Adopted_____

_____
Companion

Mark Adopted_____

_____
Companion

Mark Adopted_____

_____
Companion

Mark Adopted_____

_____
Companion

Mark Adopted_____

_____
Companion

Mark Adopted_____

_____
Companion

Mark Adopted_____

_____
Companion

Mark Adopted_____

_____
Companion

Mark Adopted_____

_____
Companion

Mark Adopted_____

_____
Companion

Mark Adopted_____

_____
Companion

Mark Adopted_____

_____
Companion

Mark Adopted_____

_____
Companion

Mark Adopted_____

_____
Companion

Mark Adopted_____

_____
Companion

Mark Adopted_____

_____
Companion

Mark Adopted_____

_____
Companion

Mark Adopted_____

_____
Companion

Mark Adopted_____

_____
Companion

Mark Adopted_____

_____
Companion

Mark Adopted_____

_____
Companion

Mark Adopted_____

_____
Companion

Mark Adopted_____

_____
Companion

Mark Adopted_____

_____
Companion

Mark Adopted_____

_____
Companion

Mark Adopted_____

_____
Companion

Mark Adopted_____

_____
Companion

Mark Adopted_____

_____
Companion

Mark Adopted_____

_____
Companion

Mark Adopted_____

_____
Companion

Mark Adopted_____

_____
Companion

Mark Adopted_____

_____
Companion

Mark Adopted_____

_____
Companion

Mark Adopted_____

_____
Companion

Mark Adopted_____

_____
Companion

Mark Adopted_____

_____
Companion

Mark Adopted_____

_____
Companion

Mark Adopted_____

_____
Companion

Mark Adopted_____

_____
Companion

Mark Adopted_____

_____
Companion

Mark Adopted_____

_____
Companion

Mark Adopted_____

_____
Companion

Mark Adopted_____

_____
Companion

Mark Adopted_____

_____
Companion

Mark Adopted_____

_____
Companion

Mark Adopted_____

_____
Companion

Mark Adopted_____

_____
Companion

Mark Adopted_____

_____
Companion

Mark Adopted_____

_____
Companion

Mark Adopted_____

_____
Companion

Mark Adopted_____

_____
Companion

Mark Adopted_____

_____
Companion

Mark Adopted_____

_____
Companion

Mark Adopted_____

_____
Companion

Mark Adopted_____

_____
Companion

Mark Adopted_____

_____
Companion

Mark Adopted_____

_____
Companion

Mark Adopted_____

_____
Companion

Mark Adopted_____

_____
Companion

Mark Adopted_____

_____
Companion

Mark Adopted_____

_____
Companion

Mark Adopted_____

_____
Companion

Mark Adopted_____

_____
Companion

Mark Adopted_____

_____
Companion

Mark Adopted_____

_____
Companion

Mark Adopted_____

_____
Companion

Mark Adopted_____

_____
Companion

Mark Adopted_____

_____
Companion

Mark Adopted_____

_____
Companion

Mark Adopted_____

_____
Companion

Mark Adopted_____

_____
Companion

Mark Adopted_____

_____
Companion

Mark Adopted_____

_____
Companion

Mark Adopted_____

_____
Companion

Mark Adopted_____

_____
Companion

Mark Adopted_____

_____
Companion

Mark Adopted_____

_____
Companion

Mark Adopted_____

_____
Companion

Mark Adopted_____

_____
Companion

Mark Adopted_____

_____
Companion

Mark Adopted_____

_____
Companion

Mark Adopted_____

_____
Companion

Mark Adopted_____

_____
Companion

Mark Adopted_____

_____
Companion

Mark Adopted_____

_____
Companion

Mark Adopted_____

_____
Companion

Mark Adopted_____

_____
Companion

Mark Adopted_____

_____
Companion

Mark Adopted_____

_____
Companion

Mark Adopted_____

_____
Companion

Mark Adopted_____

_____
Companion

Mark Adopted_____

_____
Companion

Mark Adopted_____

_____
Companion

Mark Adopted_____

_____
Companion

Mark Adopted_____

_____
Companion

Mark Adopted_____

_____
Companion

Mark Adopted_____

_____
Companion

Mark Adopted_____

_____
Companion

Mark Adopted_____

_____
Companion

Mark Adopted_____

_____
Companion

Mark Adopted_____

_____
Companion

Mark Adopted_____

_____
Companion

Mark Adopted_____

_____
Companion

Mark Adopted_____

_____
Companion

Mark Adopted_____

_____
Companion

Mark Adopted_____

_____
Companion

Mark Adopted_____

_____
Companion

Mark Adopted_____

_____
Companion

Mark Adopted_____

_____
Companion

Mark Adopted_____

_____
Companion

Mark Adopted_____

_____
Companion

Mark Adopted_____

_____
Companion

Mark Adopted_____

_____
Companion

Mark Adopted_____

_____
Companion

Mark Adopted_____

_____
Companion

Mark Adopted_____

_____
Companion

Mark Adopted_____

_____
Companion

Mark Adopted_____

_____
Companion

Mark Adopted_____

_____
Companion

Mark Adopted_____

_____
Companion

Mark Adopted_____

_____
Companion

Mark Adopted_____

_____
Companion

Mark Adopted_____

_____
Companion

Mark Adopted_____

_____
Companion

Mark Adopted_____

_____
Companion

Mark Adopted_____

_____
Companion

Mark Adopted_____

_____
Companion

Mark Adopted_____

_____
Companion

Mark Adopted_____

_____
Companion

Mark Adopted_____

_____
Companion

Mark Adopted_____

_____
Companion

Mark Adopted_____

_____
Companion

Mark Adopted_____

_____
Companion

Mark Adopted_____

_____
Companion

Mark Adopted_____

_____
Companion

Mark Adopted_____

_____
Companion

Mark Adopted_____

_____
Companion

Mark Adopted_____

_____
Companion

Mark Adopted_____

_____
Companion

Mark Adopted_____

_____
Companion

Mark Adopted_____

_____
Companion

Mark Adopted_____

_____
Companion

Mark Adopted_____

_____
Companion

Mark Adopted_____

_____
Companion

Mark Adopted_____

_____
Companion

Mark Adopted_____

_____
Companion

Mark Adopted_____

_____
Companion

Mark Adopted_____

_____
Companion

Mark Adopted_____

_____
Companion

Mark Adopted_____

_____
Companion

Mark Adopted_____

_____
Companion

Mark Adopted_____

_____
Companion

Mark Adopted_____

_____
Companion

Mark Adopted_____

_____
Companion

Mark Adopted_____

_____
Companion

Mark Adopted_____

_____
Companion

Mark Adopted_____

_____
Companion

Mark Adopted_____

_____
Companion

Mark Adopted_____

_____
Companion

Mark Adopted_____

_____
Companion

Mark Adopted_____

_____
Companion

Mark Adopted_____

_____
Companion

Mark Adopted_____

_____
Companion

Mark Adopted_____

_____
Companion

Mark Adopted_____

_____
Companion

Mark Adopted_____

_____
Companion

Mark Adopted_____

_____
Companion

Mark Adopted_____

_____
Companion

Mark Adopted_____

_____
Companion

Mark Adopted_____

_____
Companion

Mark Adopted_____

_____
Companion

Mark Adopted_____

_____
Companion

Mark Adopted_____

_____
Companion

Mark Adopted_____

_____
Companion

Mark Adopted_____

_____
Companion

Mark Adopted_____

_____
Companion

Mark Adopted_____

_____
Companion

Mark Adopted_____

_____
Companion

Mark Adopted_____

_____
Companion

Mark Adopted_____

_____
Companion

Mark Adopted_____

_____
Companion

Mark Adopted_____

_____
Companion

Mark Adopted_____

_____
Companion

Mark Adopted_____

_____
Companion

Mark Adopted_____

_____
Companion

Mark Adopted_____

_____
Companion

Mark Adopted_____

_____
Companion

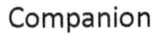

Mark Adopted_____

_____
Companion

Mark Adopted_____

_____
Companion

Mark Adopted_____

_____
Companion

Mark Adopted_____

_____
Companion

Mark Adopted_____

_____
Companion

Mark Adopted_____

_____
Companion

Mark Adopted_____

_____
Companion

Mark Adopted_____

_____
Companion

Mark Adopted_____

_____
Companion

Mark Adopted_____

_____
Companion

Mark Adopted_____

_____
Companion

Mark Adopted_____

_____
Companion

Mark Adopted_____

_____
Companion

Mark Adopted_____

_____
Companion

Mark Adopted_____

_____
Companion

Mark Adopted_____

_____
Companion

Mark Adopted_____

_____
Companion

Mark Adopted_____

_____
Companion

Mark Adopted_____

_____
Companion

Mark Adopted_____

_____
Companion

Mark Adopted_____

_____
Companion

Mark Adopted_____

_____
Companion

Mark Adopted_____

_____
Companion

Mark Adopted_____

_____
Companion

Mark Adopted_____

_____
Companion

Mark Adopted_____

_____
Companion

Mark Adopted_____

_____
Companion

Mark Adopted_____

_____
Companion

Mark Adopted_____

_____
Companion

Mark Adopted_____

_____
Companion

Mark Adopted_____

_____
Companion

Mark Adopted_____

_____
Companion

Mark Adopted_____

_____
Companion

Mark Adopted_____

_____
Companion

Mark Adopted_____

_____
Companion

Mark Adopted_____

_____
Companion

Mark Adopted_____

_____
Companion

Mark Adopted_____

_____
Companion

Mark Adopted_____

_____
Companion

Mark Adopted_____

_____
Companion

Mark Adopted_____

_____
Companion

Mark Adopted_____

_____
Companion

Mark Adopted_____

_____
Companion

Mark Adopted_____

_____
Companion

Mark Adopted_____

_____
Companion

Mark Adopted_____

_____
Companion

Mark Adopted_____

_____
Companion

Mark Adopted_____

_____
Companion

Mark Adopted_____

_____
Companion

Mark Adopted_____

_____
Companion

Mark Adopted_____

_____
Companion

Mark Adopted_____

_____
Companion

Mark Adopted_____

_____
Companion

Mark Adopted_____

_____
Companion

Mark Adopted_____

_____
Companion

Mark Adopted_____

_____
Companion

Mark Adopted_____

_____
Companion

Mark Adopted_____

_____
Companion

Mark Adopted_____

_____
Companion

Mark Adopted_____

_____
Companion

Mark Adopted_____

_____
Companion

Mark Adopted_____

_____
Companion

Mark Adopted_____

_____
Companion

Mark Adopted_____

_____
Companion

Mark Adopted_____

_____
Companion

Mark Adopted_____

_____
Companion

Mark Adopted_____

_____
Companion

Mark Adopted_____

_____
Companion

Mark Adopted_____

_____
Companion

Mark Adopted_____

_____
Companion

Mark Adopted_____

_____
Companion

Mark Adopted_____

_____
Companion

Mark Adopted_____

_____
Companion

Mark Adopted_____

_____
Companion

Mark Adopted_____

_____
Companion

Mark Adopted_____

_____
Companion

Mark Adopted_____

_____
Companion

Mark Adopted_____

_____
Companion

Mark Adopted_____

_____
Companion

Mark Adopted_____

_____
Companion

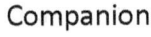

Mark Adopted_____

_____
Companion

Mark Adopted_____

_____
Companion

Mark Adopted_____

_____
Companion

Mark Adopted_____

_____
Companion

Mark Adopted_____

_____
Companion

Mark Adopted_____

_____
Companion

Mark Adopted_____

_____
Companion

Mark Adopted_____

_____
Companion

Mark Adopted_____

_____
Companion

Mark Adopted_____

_____
Companion

Mark Adopted_____

_____
Companion

Mark Adopted_____

_____
Companion

Mark Adopted_____

_____
Companion

Mark Adopted_____

_____
Companion

Mark Adopted_____

_____
Companion

Mark Adopted_____

_____
Companion

Mark Adopted_____

_____
Companion

Mark Adopted_____

_____
Companion

Mark Adopted_____

_____
Companion

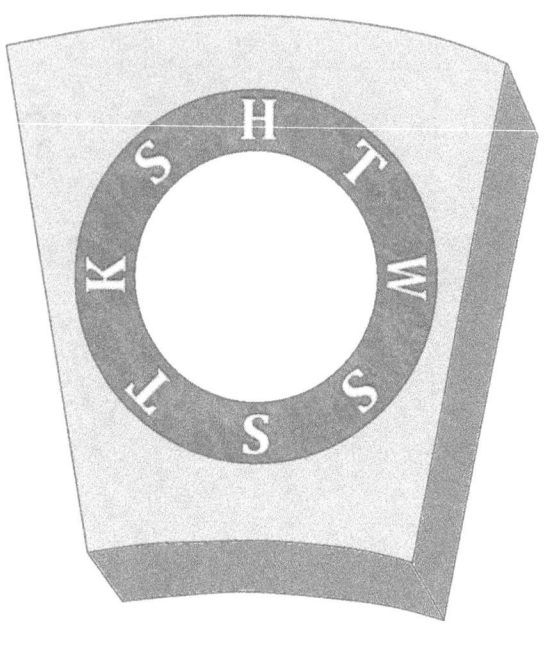

Mark Adopted_____

_____
Companion

Mark Adopted_____

_____
Companion

Mark Adopted_____

_____
Companion

Mark Adopted_____

_____
Companion

Mark Adopted_____

_____
Companion

Mark Adopted_____

_____
Companion

Mark Adopted_____

_____
Companion

Mark Adopted_____

_____
Companion

Mark Adopted_____

_____
Companion

Mark Adopted_____

_____
Companion

Mark Adopted_____

_____
Companion

Mark Adopted_____

_____
Companion

Mark Adopted_____

_____
Companion

Mark Adopted_____

_____
Companion

Mark Adopted_____

_____
Companion

Mark Adopted_____

_____
Companion

Mark Adopted_____

_____
Companion

Mark Adopted_____

_____
Companion

Mark Adopted_____

_____
Companion

Mark Adopted_____

_____
Companion

Mark Adopted_____

_____
Companion

Mark Adopted_____

_____
Companion

Mark Adopted_____

_____
Companion

Mark Adopted_____

_____
Companion

Mark Adopted_____

_____
Companion

Mark Adopted_____

_____
Companion

Mark Adopted_____

_____
Companion

Mark Adopted_____

_____
Companion

Mark Adopted_____

_____
Companion

Mark Adopted_____

_____
Companion

Mark Adopted_____

_____
Companion

Mark Adopted_____

_____
Companion

Mark Adopted_____

_____
Companion

Mark Adopted_____

_____
Companion

Mark Adopted_____

_____
Companion

Mark Adopted_____

_____
Companion

Mark Adopted_____

_____
Companion

Mark Adopted_____

_____
Companion

Mark Adopted_____

_____
Companion

Mark Adopted_____

_____
Companion

Mark Adopted_____

_____
Companion

Mark Adopted_____

_____
Companion

Mark Adopted_____

_____
Companion

Mark Adopted_____

_____
Companion

Mark Adopted_____

_____
Companion

Mark Adopted_____

_____
Companion

Mark Adopted_____

_____
Companion

Mark Adopted_____

_____
Companion

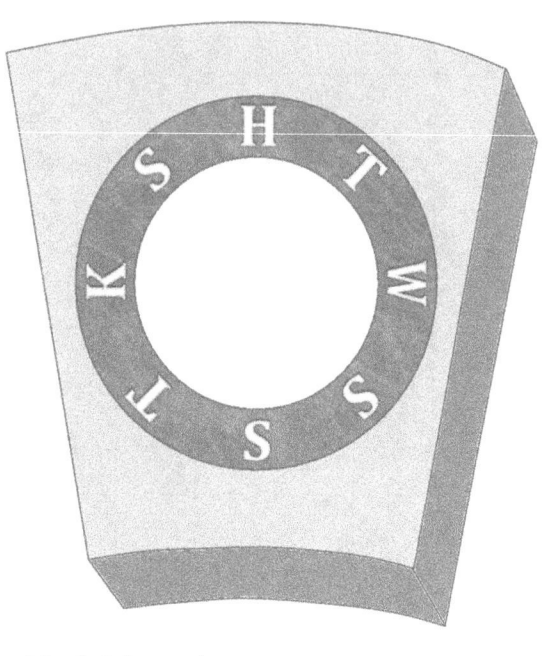

Mark Adopted_____

_____
Companion

Mark Adopted_____

_____
Companion

Mark Adopted_____

_____
Companion

Mark Adopted_____

_____
Companion

Mark Adopted_____

_____
Companion

Mark Adopted_____

_____
Companion

Mark Adopted_____

_____
Companion

Mark Adopted_____

_____
Companion

Mark Adopted_____

_____
Companion

Mark Adopted_____

_____
Companion

Mark Adopted_____

_____
Companion

Mark Adopted_____

_____
Companion

Mark Adopted_____

_____
Companion

Mark Adopted_____

_____
Companion

Mark Adopted_____

_____
Companion

Mark Adopted_____

_____
Companion

Mark Adopted_____

_____
Companion

Mark Adopted_____

_____
Companion

Mark Adopted_____

_____
Companion

Mark Adopted_____

_____
Companion

Mark Adopted_____

_____
Companion

Mark Adopted_____

_____
Companion

Mark Adopted_____

_____
Companion

Mark Adopted_____

_____
Companion

Mark Adopted_____

_____
Companion

Mark Adopted_____

_____
Companion

Mark Adopted_____

_____
Companion

Mark Adopted_____

_____
Companion

Mark Adopted_____

_____
Companion

Mark Adopted_____

_____
Companion

Mark Adopted_____

_____
Companion

Mark Adopted_____

_____
Companion

Mark Adopted_____

_____
Companion

Mark Adopted_____

_____
Companion

Mark Adopted_____

_____
Companion

Mark Adopted_____

_____
Companion

Mark Adopted_____

_____
Companion

Mark Adopted_____

_____
Companion

Mark Adopted_____

_____
Companion

Mark Adopted_____

_____
Companion

Mark Adopted_____

_____
Companion

Mark Adopted_____

_____
Companion

Mark Adopted_____

_____
Companion

Mark Adopted_____

_____
Companion

Mark Adopted_____

_____
Companion

Mark Adopted_____

_____
Companion

Mark Adopted_____

_____
Companion

Mark Adopted_____

_____
Companion

Mark Adopted_____

_____
Companion

Mark Adopted_____

_____
Companion

Mark Adopted_____

_____
Companion

Mark Adopted_____

_____
Companion

Mark Adopted_____

_____
Companion

Mark Adopted_____

_____
Companion

Mark Adopted_____

_____
Companion

Mark Adopted_____

_____
Companion

Mark Adopted_____

_____
Companion

Mark Adopted_____

_____
Companion

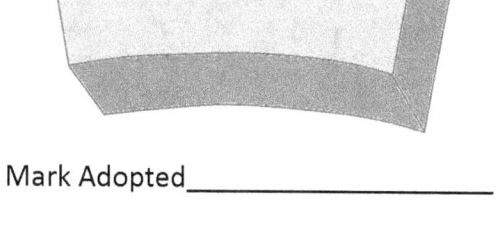

Mark Adopted_____

_____
Companion

Mark Adopted_____

_____
Companion

Mark Adopted_____

_____
Companion

Mark Adopted_____

_____
Companion

Mark Adopted_____

_____
Companion

Mark Adopted_____

_____
Companion

Mark Adopted_____

_____
Companion

Mark Adopted_____

_____
Companion

Mark Adopted_____

_____
Companion

Mark Adopted_____

_____
Companion

Mark Adopted_____

_____
Companion

Mark Adopted_____

_____
Companion

Mark Adopted_____

_____
Companion

Mark Adopted_____

_____
Companion

Mark Adopted_____

_____
Companion

Mark Adopted_____

_____
Companion

Mark Adopted_____

_____
Companion

Mark Adopted_____

_____
Companion

Mark Adopted_____

_____
Companion

Mark Adopted_____

_____
Companion

Mark Adopted_____

_____
Companion

Mark Adopted_____

_____
Companion

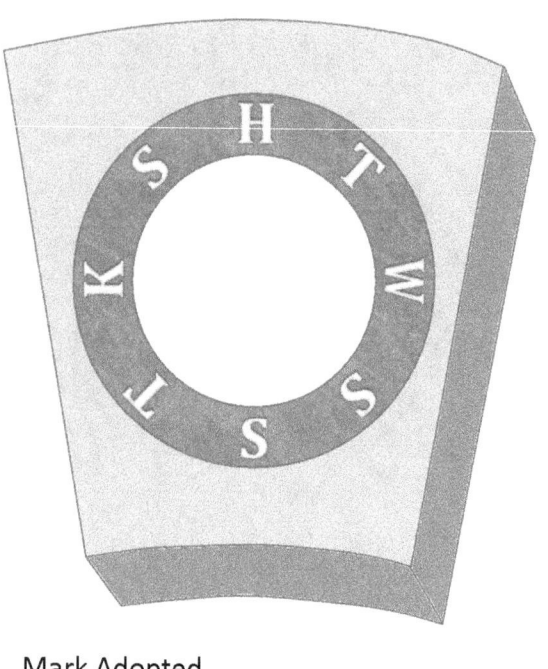

Mark Adopted_____

_____
Companion

Mark Adopted_____

_____
Companion

Mark Adopted_____

_____
Companion

Mark Adopted_____

_____
Companion

Mark Adopted_____

_____
Companion

Mark Adopted_____

_____
Companion

Mark Adopted_____

_____
Companion

Mark Adopted_____

_____
Companion

SO·MOTE·IT·BE

www.ingramcontent.com/pod-product-compliance
Lightning Source LLC
Chambersburg PA
CBHW081822280526

45789CB00007B/2302